Something To Do
(When There's Nothing To Do)

A Coloring and Activity Book
~ by Mary Engelbreit ~

Andrews and McMeel
A Universal Press Syndicate Company
Kansas City

So Much To Do

PALS

"Life has no blessing
like a good friend."

and me.

I gave this my own special touch.
With love,

_____

Valentine Punch-Outs

Use your imagination to decorate the Valentines you find here. On the back of the cards, you'll find printed messages—you can also personalize the cards with your own words. You can use the stencils at the back of the book to custom-design your own envelopes. Don't be shy about inventing your own style.

Have your fill of fun
on Valentine's Day!

Happy Valentine's Day
from
You know who!

"Sow good services;
Sweet remembrances
Will grow from them."
— Mde. de Stael

and me.

I gave this my own special touch.
With love,

_____

Painted Pots

Wouldn't it be fun to watch flowers grow from seeds in a pot that you decorated yourself? This project will help you do just that.

For the first part of this project, you'll need a clay or plastic flower pot or a wooden flower box. You can find a selection at any garden supply or hardware store, or you can use an old pot if you have one around the house. If you use an old pot, make sure that it's clean and dry before you begin.

At the bottom of this page are pictures of different kinds of flowers. To decorate your pot, you can look at these pictures and use them as guides to draw your own flowers, or you can cut these flowers out and glue them to your pot.

To draw your own flowers on your pot or box, use a pencil or felt-tip pen to sketch your design. Then, when you've got it just the way you want, use acrylic paints or crayons to color your design. (If you're using a plastic pot, permanent colored markers will probably work best.) If you want to add a border or some words to your design, you can use the stencils provided in the back of this book.

When you've finished with your design and it has completely dried, it's time to plant your flower seeds. First, place a few small rocks in the bottom of the flower pot or box. This helps extra water to drain properly from the pot. Then, fill the pot with potting soil up to about one inch from the top. Plant your seeds according to the directions on the back of the seed packet. All flowers need water and sunlight to grow, and the back of the seed packet will tell you how often to water the seeds and how much sunlight your particular flower will require.

Most seeds will start sprouting within a week or so. Once your sprouts have grown into young flowers, your decorated pots will make great gifts for parents, grandparents, and teachers.

"The goal of life
Is living in agreement
With nature."
— Zeno 335-263 B.C.

and me.

I gave this my own special touch.
With love,

_____

I gave this my own special touch.
With love,

and me.

Hope it's egg-cellent!

Easter Egg Holders

With this fun project, you'll be able to display your favorite Easter eggs for everyone to see. After you've colored and decorated your eggs, use colored pencils, markers, or crayons to decorate the Easter egg holders on this page. Then, cut out and assemble the egg holders following the directions below. You can also trace them onto other sheets of paper to create as many as you want. The stencils at the back of the book can be used to give your colorful bands the Mary Engelbreit look. Or give them your own look—whichever suits your fancy.

Create an entire centerpiece of eggs for your tabletop. Or find a cute basket, tie a ribbon around the outside, or glue a stenciled band around the outside, and fill it with straw, grass, or artificial grass. Stand your eggs up in the basket for everyone to admire.

Use your creative genius to impress the Easter Bunny with your talents!

Instructions: Cut out the egg holders along the dotted lines on the back. Follow the marks in cutting a notch at each end of the egg holder. These two notches will join to form the holder. You may want to reinforce these tabs with tape.

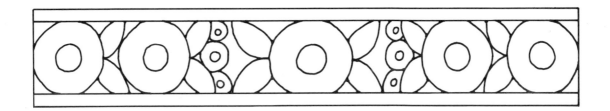

"An egg is dear on Easter Day"
— Proverb

and me.

Bookmarks and Bookplates

Bookmarks and bookplates give your books your own special touch. Two bookmarks and two bookplates are printed on this page to color, decorate, and punch out. The bookplates can be pasted at the front of your favorite books to personalize your collection.

The bookmarks can be laminated so they will last longer, and you can also punch out the holes at the top and add decorative yarn, ribbon, or string.

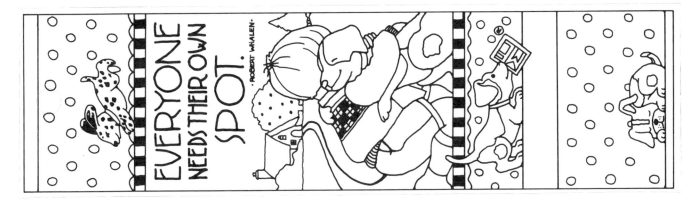

"The love of learning.
The sequestered nooks,
And all the sweet serenity of books."
— Longfellow

I gave this
my own special touch.
With love,

and me.

ME ®

I gave this
my own special touch.
With love,

and me.

ME ®

MAKE · A · WISH

and me.

I gave this my own special touch.

With love,

Hope all your birthday wishes come true!

Fancy Frames

$\bigcirc$n these pages are designs to help you create your own picture frames. These frames are measured to fit standard-size photos. Punch out the openings after you have finished decorating the frames. Place the photos on cardboard backgrounds that have been cut to fit the size of the frame. Use a glue stick or double-sided tape around the edges of the picture, and then around the edges of the frame. Press the frame over the mounted photo.

These make great gifts for Mother's Day and Father's Day. You can add an additional design or message on the back or give details of when and where the picture was taken.

Pretty as a picture!

"A picture shows me at a glance
what it takes dozens of pages of a book
to expound"
                    — Ivan Turgenev, 1862

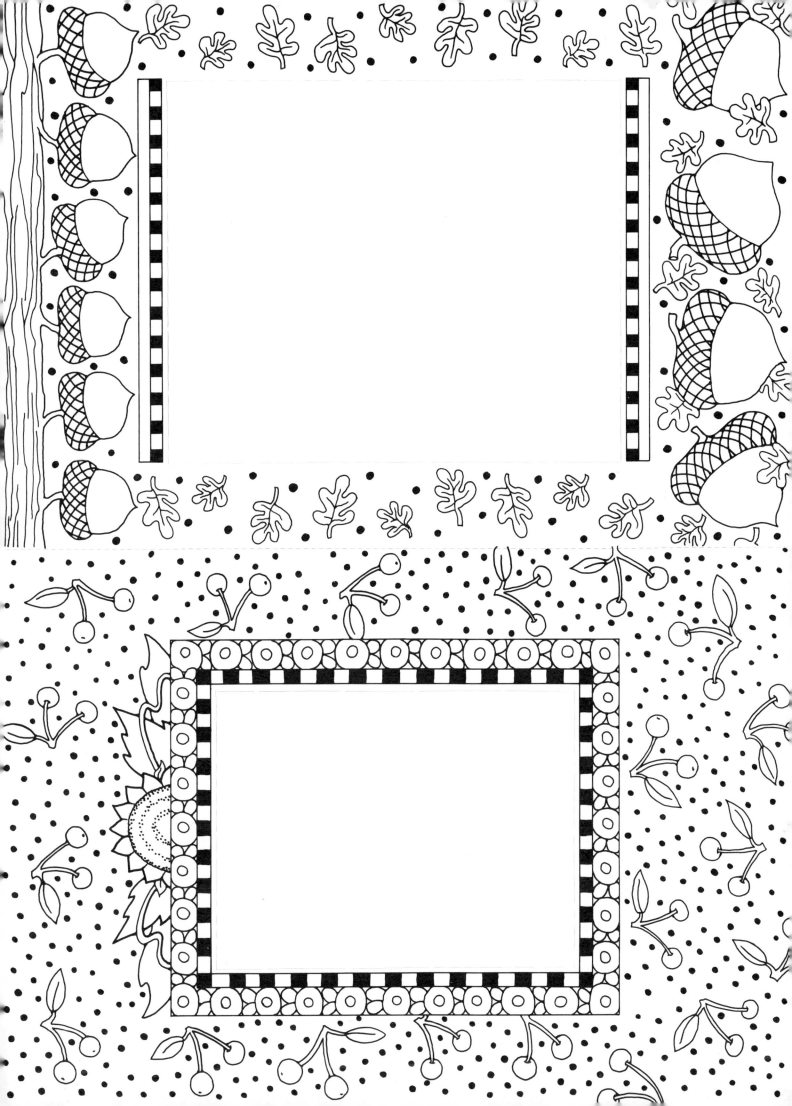

23

"Baby's fishing for a dream,
Fishing near and far,
His line a silver moonbeam is,
His bait a silver star."
— Alice C.D. Riley

and me.

I gave this my own special touch.
With love,

_____

Mobile Magic

Mobiles are very popular decorations, are easy to assemble, and make great gifts.

The easiest way to assemble this mobile is to use a clothes hanger. Choose a ribbon color and wrap it around the hanger wire to hide the metal. Glue the end pieces of ribbon in place to prevent unraveling. You may want to give the ribbon dots of glue along the way to make sure it adheres tightly to the hanger.

Each piece of art on this page has an opening for a hole punch. The decorations can be strung from the hanger using colored ribbon or string. Be sure to hang it in a spot that small children can't reach. See the diagram below for a drawing of what it looks like when assembled.

"The moon like a flower
In heaven's high bower,
With silent delight,
Sits and smiles on the night."
— William Blake

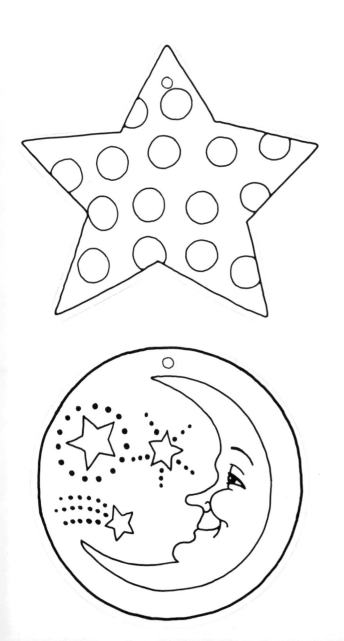

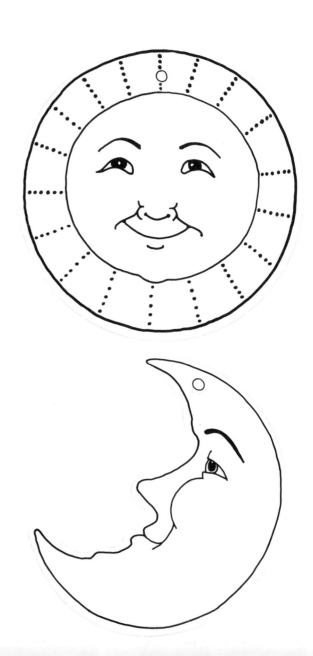

THE SIMPLE NEWS
THAT NATURE TOLD,
WITH TENDER MAJESTY

EMILY DICKINSON

"The one absolutely unselfish friend
that man can have in this selfish world
is his dog."
— George Graham Vest

and me.

I gave this my own special touch.
With love,

_____

" 'Tis now the very witching time of night."
— Shakespeare

Recipe for a Witch's Brew
Heat 1/2 gallon of apple cider on stove top.
Add a teaspoon of cinnamon and a dash of cloves to the cider.
Serve in mugs with a cinnamon stick in each.

Turn the lights low and light a jack-o'-lantern.

I gave this my own special touch.
With love,

_____

Halloween Mask

Parties, trick-or-treating, candy, and costumes—Halloween is the best! You can color the jack-o'-lantern mask below to be scary or funny. When you're finished coloring, punch out the mask and the eyes, nose, and mouth openings. Then, punch out the holes and attach string to fit around your head.

and me.

GIVE US THIS DAY OUR DAILY BREAD

and me.

I gave this my own special touch.
With love,

3

Happy Thanksgiving!

Recipe Cards

The holiday traditions of families include the food they prepare, how they present the food, and how they decorate the table. These recipe cards can be used to start a card file for your family's favorite holiday dishes.

Many people prepare food to give their friends and neighbors during the holidays. Another way to use these recipe cards is to include them with the food you've baked. You'll also find food labels on this page. These make nice decorative gift tags or can be glued to jars filled with your favorite treats.

A favorite recipe of: _____

A favorite recipe of:

Made especially for:

A favorite recipe of: _____

A favorite recipe of:

Made especially for:

"A friend may well be
reckoned the masterpiece of nature."
— Ralph Waldo Emerson

and me.

and me.

MERRILY · MERRILY

MERRILY · MERRILY

"Where children are,
there is the Golden Age."
— Novalis

and me.

I gave this my own special touch.
With love,

_____

FOR CHRISTMAS

GIVE ❤ HEART

and me.

I gave this my own special touch.
With love,

Have a Merry Christmas!

Wish List

Make your list and check it twice! On the front, Santa is holding his list of Good Children. Who is on it? Add the names that you think belong there.

On this side, there's plenty of room on the lines below to fill in your wish list and the wish lists of your family and friends.

Here's wishing you get everything you hope for!

Christmas Ornaments

Below are Mary Engelbreit ornaments that you can decorate and assemble to hang on your tree. These require a trip to the store to buy brads to attach the moveable parts of the figures. You'll need 7 brads for this project.

Color or decorate both sides, then punch them out. Match up the holes and insert the brads through the openings. Attach a colorful string or ribbon at the top to hang the ornament on your tree. To make more ornaments, you can trace the ones on this page, or create your own figures.

"At Christmas, play and make good cheer,
For Christmas comes but once a year."
— Thomas Tusser